Advent Devotions to Take You Deeper: A Season of Faith

Updated With Small Group Study Included

Laurie Hopkins

Advent Devotions to Take You Deeper

A Season of Faith

Updated With Small Group Study Included

Copyright © 2019 Laurie Hopkins

Scripture is taken from the New King James Version®. Copyright © 1982 by Thomas Nelson. Used by permission. All rights reserved.

Author Photo Credit to Julie MacDougall, Photographer at https://www.facebook.com/photographerjulie/

ISBN: 9781091472112

DEDICATION

To the One who met me on the mountain top but taught me to dance in the valley. To the One who showed me, unconditional love. To the one who spoke life into my days and purpose and destiny into my life. To the One who reminded me I was created for a unique and wonderful purpose. To the One who walks with me through this journey called life. To the One I call Lord and Savior of my life; my Precious Jesus.

CONTENTS

ACKNOWLEDGMENTS

Many thanks to my best friend, my confidante, my sweetheart, my soulmate, my husband, John, for walking this journey with me; for encouraging me along the way to step out in faith and be the woman God has called me to be.

To my family for their love and support.

To all my Spiritual moms and sisters out there who have helped me to grow into who I've become; encouraging me to be brave enough to begin using the gifts, the Father has placed within me, for His Glory.

1 INTRODUCTION:
A THREAD OF FAITH

But the just shall live by his faith. Habakkuk 2:4

The Christmas season is upon us once again. We like to see it come and inevitably, by the end of it, we love to see it go. We are a society of short attention spans and quick fixes. We like the hustle and bustle of Christmas, the decorations, the shopping, the gifts, the family and friends, the church service, the thoughts of "peace on earth, goodwill to men", the "hope" and the "mystery" of the Child born in a manager. However, we soon tire of the busyness, the excess and the time commitment and begin to look forward to new and different things. The decorations lose their sparkle, the gifts their interest and the influx of family and friends becomes tiresome. We want our old routine and schedule back.

This year we can begin to change that. This year we can look a little closer, dig a little deeper, and bring out longer-lasting truths about the Christmas season. We can strip down the complexities and find the basic truths that will hold it all together; not just while the shops and stations play Christmas music and the stores have sales, but the truths that will hold it all together and make it applicable in our daily lives long into the days, weeks and months of the next year.

The story of the birth of the Christ Child, over 2000 years ago, in a stable, in a little town called Bethlehem, is a story of many truths. It has many themes and, we are told, many implications for our lives today. But how can a story that happened that long ago be applicable to our lives today?

First and foremost the Christ Child had to be born of a woman and live 33 years on this earth as a man, in order that He could die on Calvary, taking on the sins of mankind; rising again on the third day and redeeming us by His blood, for us to have everlasting fellowship and life with the Father. There can be no Easter without Christmas. The Son of God had to become the Son of Man in order for the plan of salvation and eternal life to be completed.

> "For unto us a Child is born, unto us a Son is given; and the government will be upon His shoulder. And His name will be called Wonderful, Counselor, Mighty God, Everlasting Father, Prince of Peace. Of the increase of His government and peace there

will be no end, upon the throne of
David and over His kingdom, to
order it and establish it with
judgment and justice from that time
forward, even forever. The zeal of
the Lord of hosts will perform
this." (Isaiah 9:6-7).

"Jesus spoke these words, lifted up
His eyes to heaven, and said,
'Father, the hour has come. Glorify
Your Son, that Your Son may also
glorify You, as You have given Him
authority over all flesh, that He
should give eternal life to as many
as You have given Him. And this is
eternal life, that they may know
You, the only true God, and Jesus
Christ, whom You have sent. I
have glorified You on the earth. I
have finished the work which You
have given Me to do. And now, O
Father, glorify Me together with
Yourself, with the glory which I
had with You before the world
was.'" (John 17:1-5).

This is THE thread of truth that runs through all the other messages of the season and brings it all together; weaving together a story of peace, goodwill, love and hope. But there is another truth that I would like to share with you this Christmas season. A truth that may help us to understand why Christmas is much more than what many of us have come to expect and settle for.

Let's consider the stories of each individual involved in the Christmas narrative: Mary, Joseph, Zacharias, Elizabeth, the Wise Men, the Shepherds, Simeon and Anna, the Chief Priests and Scribes, and Herod. There are so many individuals, each with an individual part in the birth of Christ. When you look closely at each life, what thread knits them together? Why has each one's involvement granted them a place in the Word of God, a part of one of the most amazing accounts of all time?

I would suggest that the thread that brings them all together is faith. The Christmas story is a story of faith; faith in many forms, many shapes and many sizes. We read of great faith, little faith, faith by sight, faith in science, faith in self, and faith in the promises of God.

The Word defines faith this way: "Now faith is the substance of things hoped for, the evidence of things not seen." (Hebrews 11:1). Basically, faith is being able to look beyond what you see in your circumstance right now, to what could or might be. How does that apply to my life, you ask? What does this have to do with me? Have you ever thought about Christmas as a season of faith? Have you ever considered your own faith? Have you ever thought about what you have faith in, what kind of faith you have, or if you have any faith at all? Have you ever thought about the impact of your faith on your attitude, your decision-making, your well-being, and your everyday life? Have you ever wondered why, for many of us, Christmas has become just another holiday instead of the God-given example of faith, love, and hope that it truly is?

Join us as we consider Christmas as a season of faith; as we look at the faith stories of the various individuals involved in the Christmas account. As we do so, I would ask that you consider some of the following questions: How does your faith impact the celebration of Christmas? Do you have faith in the truth of the birth of the Christ Child? Do you have faith in the hope that that birth brings forth?

I believe that an understanding of faith may bring back the sparkle of the Christmas season. That we may be able to begin to peel away the rush and complexity and the disappointment that we often feel after the season and bring back to our lives, and the lives of those we love, the simplicity and hope that the first Christmas epitomized.

Let us pray together:

Almighty God, Giver of hope, love and life itself; we praise Your holy name and thank You for this Christmas season – the season in which we celebrate the birth of the Christ Child – the first step on the road to Calvary and eternal life. Although some of us would be hesitant to admit it, for many of us the Christmas season has lost its meaning and we have been left with a time of rush and excess and stress that leaves us empty and disappointed in the end. We long, Father, for the meaning and simplicity of earlier times. We aren't exactly sure where we took the wrong turn or how to find our way back. We ask, Father, that you would grant us wisdom and understanding this Christmas season as we search Your Word and study the lives of faith of those involved in the events of the first Christmas. Grant us, divine revelation Father. Show us Your truth. Help us to examine our faith and its impact on how we celebrate the birth of Your Son as well as its impact on our daily lives long after Christmas has passed. We bring these things before You in the precious name of Jesus. Amen and Amen and Amen.

2 FIRST SUNDAY OF ADVENT: SIGN OR SURRENDER

"And Zacharias said to the angel, 'How shall I know this? For I am an old man, and my wife is well advanced in years.'" (Luke 1:18).

"Then Mary said, 'Behold the maidservant of the Lord! Let it be to me according to your word.' And the angel departed from her."(Luke 1:38)

The Christmas story as recorded in Luke tells us that an angel of God appeared to both Mary and Zacharias, bringing them the news that they were to be involved in the Christmas miracle. Let's begin with an understanding of who these individuals were, what their circumstances were, and the message they received from the angel Gabriel.

The Background

Zacharias: Luke tells us that Zacharias was a priest, married to Elizabeth who was of the daughters of Aaron and that "they were both righteous before God, walking in all the commandments and ordinances of the Lord blameless. But they had no child because Elizabeth was barren, and they were both well advanced in years." (Luke 1: 6-7). Zacharias served as a priest before God, and at this time his "lot fell to burn incense when he went into the temple of God." (Luke 1: 9). It is important to note that the burning of the incense was something that a priest did only once in his lifetime. The timing of the Lord is always AWESOME!

Mary: Luke tells us that Mary was "a virgin, betrothed to a man whose name was Joseph, of the house of David." (Luke 1: 27) and they were from a small town in the city of Galilee, Nazareth. Luke tells us nothing of her belief, status or circumstances in life, but we can assume from the overall story that she was a young girl, from a simple background.

The Message

Zacharias: As Zacharias entered the temple of the Lord to burn incense, an angel of the Lord appeared to him.

> "Do not be afraid, Zacharias, for your
> prayer is heard; and your wife
> Elizabeth will bear you a son, and you
> shall call his name John. And you will

have joy and gladness, and many will
rejoice at his birth. For he will be
great in the sight of the Lord and shall
drink neither wine nor strong drink.
He will also be filled with the Holy
Spirit even from his mother's womb.
And he will turn many of the children
of Israel to the Lord their God. He
will also go before Him in the spirit
and power of Elijah, 'to turn the
hearts of the fathers to their children'
and the disobedient to the wisdom of
the just, to make ready a people
prepared for the Lord." (Luke 1: 13-
17).

Mary: The angel Gabriel begins his conversation with Mary by
stating,

"Rejoice, highly favored one, the Lord
is with you; blessed are you among
woman!" (Luke 1:28) and continues,
"Do not be afraid, Mary, for you have
found favor with God. And behold
you will conceive in your womb and
bring forth a Son, and shall call His
name Jesus. He will be great, and will

be called the Son of the Highest; and the Lord God will give Him the throne of His father David. And He will reign over the house of Jacob forever, and of His kingdom there will be no end." (Luke 1:30-33).

"The Holy Spirit will come upon you, and the power of the Highest will overshadow you; therefore, also, that Holy One who is to be born will be called the Son of God. Now indeed, Elizabeth your relative has also conceived a son in her old age, and this is now the sixth month for her who was called barren. For with God nothing will be impossible." (Luke 1: 35-37).

The Response

Zacharias: When Zacharias saw Gabriel, we are told, "he was troubled and fear fell upon him" (Luke 1: 12). Zacharias was assured that there was no need to fear and the message was given. "Zacharias said to the angel, 'How shall I know this? For I am an old man, and my wife is well advanced in years." (Luke 1:18). Zacharias asked for a sign from God. In response to his request for a sign, Gabriel identifies himself as one "who stands in the presence of God" (Luke 1: 19) and tells Zacharias that because of his unbelief he will be mute until the day that "these things take place." (Luke 1: 20).

Mary: Upon receiving the initial greeting from Gabriel we are told that Mary "was troubled at his saying, and considered what manner of greeting this was" (Luke 1: 29) but there is no mention of fear. Upon receiving the message Mary seeks understanding of the message, "'how can this be, since I do not know a man?'" (Luke 1: 34). In her final response, Mary humbles herself and surrenders herself to the will of God. "'Behold the maidservant of the Lord! Let it be to me according to your word.'" (Luke 1: 38).

Now that we know the story, let us consider it through the lens of faith. Zacharias is a priest, serving God for many years, considered righteous in the sight of God, along with Elizabeth his wife, who is of the daughters of Aaron. Zacharias has prayed to God for a child, yet he and his wife are described as advanced in years and his wife is called barren.

The angel Gabriel has come to tell Zacharias that his prayers have not only been heard but are about to be answered. Elizabeth will bear a son and many will rejoice over his birth. Furthermore, their son will be great in the sight of the Lord, will be filled with the Holy Spirit, will fulfill prophecy, and prepare the way for his Lord! WOW! What a message! What joyous promises Gabriel delivers to Zacharias; on this one precious day, as a priest of the Lord, that he comes to the temple to burn incense before God

This is a message of hope and joy. There is no expectation of either he or his wife, just to accept the answered prayer and rejoice in it. The reproach of Elizabeth who has been called barren will be removed and all will know that it has been by the Hand of God; a miracle. Zacharias will have his son and can rejoice in the knowledge that his son will fulfill the prophecy of the scriptures, that the God that Zacharias has spent his life serving will use his son to prepare the way for the coming Lord!

What does Zacharias do with this message? He questions God. He asks for a sign; a sign from God that this Angel of the Lord is telling the truth. He, who sees the vision with his own eyes, receives the message with his own ears and has nothing to lose and everything to gain by the fulfillment of this message, asks God for a sign.

Mary, on the other hand, is a young girl. The angel Gabriel comes before her and tells her to rejoice for she is highly favoured, the Lord is with her and she is blessed among women. The message starts off well. But then he tells her that she will conceive a Child. Not any Child, but a Son, the Son of the Highest; He will have the throne of David and will reign forever, with no end to His Kingdom. This Child will be conceived within her body by the Holy Spirit and will be the Son of God!

This is also a message of hope, joy, prophecy fulfilled; the arrival of the Messiah! BUT this message requires MUCH of Mary, unlike the message to Zacharias. This message requires that Mary surrender her body to the Holy Spirit and allow the conception of the

Son of God to occur. WOW! Now we must remember Mary is a young, unmarried girl. She has not known a man, but she is about to be made visibly pregnant. What will her betrothed think, her parents, and the people around her? Will she be labelled an adulteress, shamed, shunned and even stoned for her sin? Who will believe that she is carrying the Son of God?

Furthermore, this is the Son of Almighty God! Imagine the responsibility that is being placed upon her young shoulders, her tender mind and spirit, and her physical body; the expectation that she will bear within her the Son of God and then raise the Son of God, from a baby to a man.

What is Mary's response? Her response is twofold. Initially, she asks of Gabriel, "How can this be, since I do not know a man?" (Luke 1: 34). This is not a doubting question but rather a question of one who seeks understanding, rather than a sign. In asking for understanding, Gabriel offers her the two things she hasn't asked for: 1) A sign – Elizabeth who has been called barren has been with child for six months 2) Reassurance - with God nothing will be impossible. What does Mary so with this message? "Behold, the maidservant of the Lord! Let it be to me according to your word." (Luke 1: 38). Words of simple faith and complete and total surrender!

Consider your own faith for a moment. In what ways are you like Zacharias and in what ways are you like Mary? Has your faith required much of you or little? Has that affected whether you have been accepting of the Voice of God or whether you required repeated messages and signs from the Father? Do you know what you believe in? Do you seek to understand the things of God that you don't understand? Or do you just lay out your fleece again and again as the Father speaks to you and asks you to surrender your life to His will and His plan and purpose?

Do you have trouble believing that anyone would have faith that would allow them to simply believe and surrender to God as Mary did, despite the potential consequences for her? Do you have difficulty believing that anyone would question God rather than jumping to their feet and praising the Father for answering their prayer in such a powerful way, as Zacharias did?

What does your faith cost you? Mary's faith cost her everything, complete surrender; but the Lord carried her. Zacharias's faith would have cost him nothing, but his lack of faith cost him the ability to speak until after his son was born and the Word of God had been fulfilled.

What is God asking you to believe and/or do, in faith, this Christmas Season? Less hustle and bustle, more quiet time with Him? Less of the world's Christmas and more of the simplicity of the message of hope, love and faith? Less concern about keeping up with the neighbours and more time teaching your children what Christmas really is about: hope, love, family, friends, fellowship, and the birth of the Christ Child. Is He asking you to step out of your comfort zone and reach out His hand of love or hope, through you and your family, this Christmas Season?

Ask the Lord of all faith, hope and love to guide you, to speak to you, and to open up your mind and spirit to hear His Words as you take time to listen to Him this Christmas season; as you seek to really UNDERSTAND what Christmas is all about!

<u>Let us pray together:</u>

Gracious Father of all faith, hope and love, we come and sit still before you as we prepare for this Christmas season. We have lost our way and we seek Your direction to find Your path among the paths of the world. We thank you, for the most precious gift of all time, Your Beloved Son, whom You sent to earth in the form of a baby in Bethlehem. This was the first step of a journey that would lead to Calvary where He would shed His blood for our salvation. We ask Father that you would speak to us; show us the journey back to the true message of Christmas. The message that is not just for a season but one that we should live out every day of our lives; through our bodies, minds, and spirits, an extension of Your Almighty Hand in this world. We Praise Your Almighty Name as we bring these things before you in the Name of Jesus. Amen and Amen and Amen!

3 SECOND SUNDAY OF ADVENT:
SENSES AND SERVING

How are you enjoying this Season of Faith? Have you been listening
to the Voice of God? Has He been sharing the message of hope,
love and faith with you in new ways? Are you excited to be on this
journey? I am! And I'm excited to be sharing it with you.

Now, let's look at 4 more individuals in the Christmas message;
Joseph, Elizabeth, Simeon and Anna, and their unique faith lens.

++++++++

Joseph

Do You Hear What I Hear?

"Then Joseph, being aroused from sleep, did as the angel of the Lord
commanded him and took to him his wife, and did not know her till
she has brought forth her firstborn son. And he called His name
Jesus." (Matthew 1:24, 25).

Let's start with Joseph. What do we know about him? Based on the genealogy given in the first chapter of Matthew, we know that Joseph was a direct descendant of David. We know that he was from Nazareth in Galilee and that he was betrothed to Mary. We see throughout the Christmas message that he was a man who heard from God and who was obedient to God. We repeatedly hear God giving Joseph direction and Joseph following without question.

To begin with, God tells him not to be afraid but to take Mary as his wife, "For that which is conceived in her is of the Holy Spirit." (Matthew 2:20). Despite the potential for shame and to be shunned for taking Mary as his wife, as she was pregnant before they were married, Joseph was obedient to the Voice of God. Joseph and Mary travelled to Bethlehem to be registered and while there she delivered her Child, in a stable, as "there was no room for them in the inn" (Luke 2:7). After the birth of the Child, God directed Joseph 3 times with regard to where they were to go: 1) "Arise, take the young Child and His mother, flee to Egypt, and stay there until I bring you word; for Herod will seek the young Child to destroy Him." (Matthew 2:13). 2) "Arise, take the young Child and His mother, and go to the land of Israel, for those who sought the young Child's life are dead." (Matthew 2:20). 3) "And being warned by God in a dream, he turned aside into the region of Galilee." (Matthew 2: 22).

Each time we are told that Joseph heard the Voice of God, and in faith, responded in obedience. He was attuned to the Voice of God and as he continued to be obedient God continued to speak direction into his life. Jesus says "My sheep hear My voice, and I know them, and they follow Me." (John 10:27) Joseph knew His God and His Shepherd. Joseph was also obedient to God's call on his life to raise a child who was not his son; a child that was the very Son of God. Joseph didn't question what he heard or Whom he heard speaking, by simple faith he walked in obedience.

+++++++

Elizabeth

I Will Praise Him!

"Now after those days his wife Elizabeth conceived; and she hid herself five months, saying 'Thus the Lord has dealt with me, in the days when He looked on me, to 'Take away my reproach among people'".

(Luke 1: 24, 25).

Elizabeth, the wife of Zacharias, was advanced in age and called barren. After her husband hears from Gabriel, the Angel of the Lord, and returns home from his service as a priest in the temple, Elizabeth conceives a child. How amazing that this woman who was advanced in age and was called barren conceived; truly a miracle of Almighty God! The Word does not tell us what Zacharias shared with his wife regarding his encounter in the temple. All we are told is that Elizabeth did indeed conceive.

When she conceived, "she hid herself away five months: (Luke 1:24) and she praised her God. She acknowledged the Hand of the

Lord in her conception and praised Him for taking away her reproach. She did not question God, "Why at my age did you give me a child?", "Why did you not answer our prayers earlier?", "Why did you allow me to live shamed among my people for so long without a child," Instead, Elizabeth accepted that the Lord had blessed her with a child and praised Him without question. What a blessing it is to be able to accept and praise the Lord in faith! As part of her sign from the Angel, Mary was told of Elizabeth's pregnancy. Mary went to visit Elizabeth.

"And it happened when
Elizabeth heard the greeting
of Mary, that the babe leaped
in her womb; and Elizabeth
was filled with the Holy
Spirit. Then she spoke out
with a loud voice and said,
"Blessed are you among
women, and blessed is the
fruit of your womb! But why
is this granted to me, that the
mother of my Lord should
come to me? For indeed, as
soon as the voice of your
greeting sounded in my ears,
the babe leaped in my womb

for joy. Blessed is she who
believed, for there will be a
fulfillment of those things
which were told her from the
Lord." (Luke 1:41-45).

The Word tells us that the Lord is enthroned (or inhabits) the praises of His people. "But You are holy, enthroned in the praises of Israel" (Psalm 22:3). Elizabeth had been praising God and now we see her filled with the Holy Spirit as her son testified of his Lord, even from the womb. We are not given any indication that Elizabeth knew that Mary was carrying the Christ Child. But the revelation of God allowed her to speak a blessing on Mary and the "fruit of her womb", as she marvelled and praised God for allowing her to play a role in His great plan. "But why is this granted to me, that the mother of my Lord should come to me?" Elizabeth's faith in acceptance and praise led to the Presence of the Holy Spirit and revelation from God.

++++++++

Simeon

Seeing is Believing

"Lord, now You are letting Your servant depart in peace, according to Your Word; for my eyes have seen Your salvation." (Luke 2:29, 30).

Simeon, we are told, "was just and devout, waiting for the Consolation of Israel, and the Holy Spirit was upon him. And it had been revealed to him by the Holy Spirit that he would not see death before he had seen the Lord's Christ." (Luke 2:25, 26). We are not told that Simeon was serving in the temple, but that he came to the temple. We understand that he was an everyday citizen who received a promise from God. The Word tells us that:

> "He came by the Spirit into
> the temple. And when the
> parents brought in the Child,
> Jesus, to do for Him
> according to the customs of
> the law, he took Him up in
> his arms and blessed God
> and said: 'Lord, now You are
> letting Your servant depart in
> peace, according to Your
> Word; for my eyes have seen
> Your salvation which You
> have prepared before the face
> of all peoples, a light to bring
> revelation to the Gentiles,
> and the glory of Your people
> Israel." (Luke 2:27-32).

Simeon received a promise from God that he would see the salvation of God before his death. Simeon's faith allowed him to live out his everyday life while waiting for the promise of God. God fulfilled that promise by allowing Simeon to see the Child Jesus. Simeon blessed God and acknowledged the fulfillment of God's promise.

Yet Simeon had only seen the Child. He has not seen the fulfillment of Jesus' 33 years on earth, his death on the cross, shed blood, or resurrection. Yet Simeon, in faith, and through the revelation of God, believed that this Child, Jesus, Who was in the temple, WOULD be the fulfillment of the salvation of the Lord.

He waited in faith on the promise of God and he would CONTINUE to wait in faith, that the Lord would bring that promise to fulfillment through the Child He held in his arms. He was willing to accept that this would happen after "he depart[ed] in peace."

The faith of Simeon could be paralleled to the faith of Abraham and his descendants. Abraham left his country in faith and obedience to the command of God.

> "Abram dwelt in the land of
> Canaan…and the Lord said
> to Abram, after Lot had
> separated from him: 'Lift
> your eyes now and look from
> the place where you are –
> northward, southward,

eastward, and westward; for
all the land which you see I
give to you and your
descendants forever. And I
will make your descendants
as the dust of the earth; so
that if a man could number
the dust of the earth, then
your descendants also could
be numbered. Arise, walk in
the land through its length
and its width, for I give it to
you. "(Genesis 13:12-17).

God promised Abraham descendants as numerous as the "dust of the earth", although Abraham was advanced in age and his wife Sarah was barren. God also promised Abraham that the land of Canaan would be his. Abraham walked in faith in his everyday life and God showed Abraham and Sarah the beginning of the fulfillment of the promise in the birth of their son Isaac. But neither Isaac nor his son Jacob saw the fulfillment of the ownership of the land of Canaan. And yet we read in Hebrews that: "These all died in faith, not having received the promises, but having seen them afar off were assured of them, embraced them and confessed that they were strangers and pilgrims on the earth" (Hebrews 11:13).

Likewise, Simeon's faith allowed him to live through his everyday life while waiting for the promise of God. When God showed him just the beginning of that promise, in the Child, Jesus, Simeon's faith allowed him to be assured of the fulfillment of that promise, although afar off and beyond his own days and sight.

++++++++

Anna

Yet Will I Serve Him!

"And coming in that instant she gave thanks to the Lord, and spoke of Him to all those who looked for redemption in Jerusalem." (Luke 2:38).

Anna was a Prophetess of God. She knew of the prophecy of the Messiah and the redemption He would bring to God's people. We are told she was "a widow of about eighty-four years, who did not depart from the temple, but served God with fastings and prayers, night and day." (Luke 2:37). Like Simeon, Anna's faith was one that waited on the promise of God. Anna's faith was also one of a lifetime of service, serving her God in the temple day and night.

In her faith and dedication to God, God revealed the fulfillment of the prophecy to her in "that instant". She immediately recognized the fulfillment of the promise and began to give God thanks and to spread the "good news" that redemption had come. "And coming in that instant she gave thanks to the Lord, and spoke of Him to all those who looked for redemption in Jerusalem." (Luke 2:38).

Anna's faith allowed her to dedicate her life, day and night, to the Lord, as she waited on the promise of a Savior. Her faith also enabled her to be open to receive the gift of the revelation of the fulfillment, give praise to God and begin to share the good news.

+++++++

Where is your faith this Christmas Season? As you continue to seek a renewed meaning in the Christmas message, may you find the faith that hears and obeys, the faith that accepts and praises, the faith that waits on the promise in everyday life, and the faith that serves as it waits; that your faith would lead you to KNOW the Voice of God, receive the Presence of the Holy Spirit, trust in the fulfillment of the promise although afar off and receive the revelation of Almighty God.

Let us pray together:

Heavenly Father, He who speaks, fulfills, and reveals, we come before You and cry Holy, Holy, Holy, Lord God Almighty! We are humbled in Your presence this Christmas season as we seek to learn the faith story. We are humbled by these men and women whose lives You have chosen to be part of the miracle of the birth of the Christ Child. We are humbled by their faith, their obedience, their praise and their service – but we are even more humbled by the thought that you choose to record their stories in Your Word, that we might know and understand that you have also chosen each one of us, as "every day" as we may be. We know that this journey into faith impacts much more than how we spend our Christmas this year; that it impacts how we live our very lives. We know that you have a plan for each of our lives and we ask as we continue on this journey of faith, that you would grant us wisdom regarding our own faith, where it is and where it needs to be and how to walk that path; that you would reveal to us Your plan for our lives and would grant us the faith to walk it out in obedience and service. We ask this in the precious Name of Jesus, the Christ. Amen and Amen and Amen.

4 THIRD SUNDAY OF ADVENT: FAITH AND SIGHT

How are you enjoying our journey through Christmas as a season of faith? Are you gaining new insights into the faith of those that were involved in the Christmas message? Are you learning about your own faith? Let's continue by looking through the faith lens of the Shepherds, the Wise Men, the chief priests and scribes and Herod the King.

++++++++

Shepherds

Do You See What I See?

"Then the angel said to them, 'Do not be afraid, for behold, I bring you good tidings of great joy which will be to all people. For there is born to you this day in the city of David a Savior, which is Christ the Lord. And this will be the sign to you: you will find a Babe wrapped in swaddling cloths, lying in a manger.'"

Luke 2:10-12

We find the shepherds out in the countryside, minding their own business, tending to their sheep, when all of a sudden they are treated to the show of a lifetime. An Angel of the Lord appears to them, the glory of the Lord shines all around them and the Angel delivers a Message of great hope and joy! And then the heavenly choir shows up: "suddenly there was with the angel a multitude of the heavenly host praising God and saying: Glory to God in the highest, and on earth peace, goodwill toward men!'" (Luke 2: 13, 14). WOW!

The Shepherds don't question the appearance of the Angel or the heavenly host, and they accept the message as coming from God, but they do decide they want to see this thing for themselves. "The shepherds said to one another, 'Let us now go to Bethlehem and see this thing that has come to pass, which the Lord as made known to us.'" (Luke 2: 15). So they took their sheep and headed to Bethlehem where they found the Baby. "Now when they had seen Him, they made widely known the saying which was told them concerning this Child…then the shepherds returned, glorifying and praising God, for all the things that they had heard and seen, as it was told them." (Luke 2: 17, 20).

So what can we say of the faith of the shepherds? The shepherds did not question the message or the Messenger, amazing as the show was! They accepted it but then sought to see for themselves. They listened, heard God speak through the Angel, and they picked up their belongings and sought after the Christ Child. Once they had seen the Babe they made known to others what they had HEARD and SEEN and been TOLD, while glorifying and praising God.

We could say that the shepherds had faith that believed and sought to SEE and HEAR more of what they had been told. Theirs was a faith of seeking, and sight, but also a faith that spread the "good news" enthusiastically once they had seen!

++++++++

Wise Men

Do You Know What I Know?

Behold wise men from the East came to Jerusalem, saying 'Where is He who has been born King of the Jews? For we have seen His star in the East and have come to worship Him?'"

Matthew 2:1, 2

The wise men were astrologers who came seeking to find the King of the Jews based on a new star that had appeared in the heavens. They travelled a great distance to come to Jerusalem, having faith that the star singled the birth of the Christ Child. Their intention was to come and worship the new King and to bring treasures to him. Their faith was based on knowledge; knowledge of the constellations; knowledge of prophecy; knowledge of travel. Their faith demanded commitment; commitment of study, time, travel and treasure and even commitment to courage in approaching the current King of Jerusalem to ask about the birth of a new King.

They were rewarded for their faith. "And when they had come into the house, they saw the young Child with Mary His mother, and fell down and worshiped Him. And when they had opened their treasures, they presented gifts to Him: gold, frankincense, and myrrh." (Matthew 2:11). The wise men also heard from God and were obedient to His voice. They were warned in a dream not to return to Jerusalem to Herod and so "they departed for their country another way." (Matthew 2:12).

The faith of the wise men was a faith-based on knowledge. A logical faith based on putting the pieces together and seeing the whole picture. And once they KNEW what they believed, they moved forward with great commitment to find and worship the Child. They also had a faith of obedience to the Voice of God.

++++++++

The Chief Priests and Scribes

Blinded by the Darkness

"And this is the condemnation, that the light has come into the world, and men loved darkness rather than light because their deeds were evil."

John 3:19

The chief priests and scribes were the leadership of the Church of that day. They were to bring direction to the people. They knew of the prophecy of the Messiah. In fact when King Herod consulted them as to where the "Christ was to be born" they answered without hesitation, "In Bethlehem of Judea, for thus it is written by the prophet:" (Matthew 2:5). And yet we read that they were troubled by the query of the wise men regarding the newborn King of the Jews. "Herod the king…was troubled, and all Jerusalem with him." (Matthew 2: 3). After that, we read no more about the chief priests and scribes in the remainder of this Christmas message. Where were they? You would have thought that they would be rejoicing and dancing in the street. The star and the wise men that followed after it was an indication of the fulfillment of the prophecy of the coming Messiah.

What of their faith? They knew the prophecy; one thinks that if they believed the prophecy they would be eager to follow the wise men or to ask them to return and share their findings with them.

John 3 tells us that when the Light came into the world that men loved darkness because their deeds were evil, and therefore they hid from the Light. In Jesus' later years of Ministry, He would spend much time speaking out against this group of church leaders for their hypocrisy and their love of the approval of man rather than that of God. One could suggest that although they had a belief, that their eyes were blinded to the truth. As the Christ Child (the Light) came into the world they choose darkness.

++++++++

King Herod

Self-Faith

"Then Herod, when he saw that he was deceived by the wise men, was exceedingly angry, and he sent forth and put to death all the male children who were in Bethlehem and in all its districts, from two years old and under, according to the time which he had determined from the wise men."

Matthew 2:16

Herod was the King of all Palestine and his reign was known for its terror and bloodshed. Imagine being approached by the wise men, inquiring about the newborn King of the Jews. What courage they had and what anger they instilled within him with their query. Herod quickly consulted the chief priests and scribes as to where the Christ was to be born. Being very crafty he gave that information to the wise men and encouraged them to return to Jerusalem with news of the Child so that he could also go and worship him. No doubt he thought he would allow the wise men to do the work, find the Child, and then take care of Him quickly. When his plan failed and the wise men did not return he did not hesitate to take matters into his own hands and ordered the very public and brutal massacre of all male children in Bethlehem, under the age of 2 years.

So what of Herod's faith? Did he have faith? Well, he definitely had belief. He believed the wise men and the quest for the Child and he believed the prophecy as quoted by the chief priests and scribes that the Christ would be born in Bethlehem. He also believed that this Christ Child would become the King of the Jews. Otherwise, he would not have taken such drastic measures to protect himself. Why did he not rejoice in the fulfillment of the prophecy, that the Savior would come and rule His people and His people would be free? Did he care about the freedom of the people, or was his only interest for himself, his own life and his status/position as King? What did Herod have faith in? Herod had self-faith. Herod believed that he was able to thwart the very plan of Almighty God.

Herod's faith was nothing more than arrogance; faith that he, as an individual, could take care of the situation even to the point of stopping the Savior from coming to rule His people; a plan that has been in place since before the beginning of time.

What of your faith? Do you have faith to see and hear more and then spread the good news? Or is your faith more of the "once I know I will make the commitment"? Or perhaps like the chief scribes and Pharisees, you find yourself blinded by the darkness. Or like Herod, you may find your faith only in yourself and your ability to make things happen. As we approach the fourth week of Advent, this is a good time to think about what type of faith you have and what you have faith in.

<u>Let us pray together:</u>

Heavenly Father, Giver of light, knowledge and faith itself, we come before you and thank you for this opportunity to see Your direction and guidance in this Advent season. Once again we acknowledge that the sparkle of Christmas has dulled and we wish to regain our joy and faith in the Christmas season. Awaken our desire to see and hear more of what you have for us while not relying on our knowledge or our ability to take care of things ourselves. Keep us from being blinded by the darkness and help us to choose the light, even the very Light of Your Son, Jesus Christ, in whom we pray. Amen and Amen and Amen.

5 FOURTH SUNDAY OF ADVENT: THE MEANING IN THE MESSAGE

And it came to pass in those days
that a decree went out from Caesar
Augustus that all the world should
be registered. This census first took
place while Quirinius was governing
Syria. So all went to be registered,
everyone to his own city. Joseph
also went up from Galilee, out of
the city of Nazareth, into Judea, to
the city of David, which is called
Bethlehem, because he was of the
house and lineage of David, to be
registered with Mary, his betrothed
wife, who was with child. So it was,
that while they were there, the days
were completed for her to be

delivered. And she brought forth her firstborn Son, and wrapped Him in swaddling clothes, and laid Him in a manger, because there was no room for them in the inn. Luke 2: 1-7

Throughout the last few weeks we have seen faith through the lens of many individuals and groups; so many types of faith, changing with time and circumstances. Are you able to identify with any of them as you peer through their lens of faith?

What is God asking you to do, in faith, today? Will it cost you little like Zacharias? Will it cost you much, like Mary? Will you continue to ask for a sign or are you ready to surrender?

Are you in tune with the Voice of your Shepherd, ready to take His direction, like Joseph? Are you ready to praise Him for His Hand in your life, like Elizabeth, leading to continued revelation? Are you willing, in your everyday life to wait on the promises of God leading to further revelation and hope, as Simeon and Anna experienced?

Are you one who needs to SEE for yourself and then are ready to run with the Word of the Lord? Are you one who works the puzzle logically? Do you have a great commitment to the cost of seeking the Lord; time, knowledge, and treasures?

Have you ever had a time when your faith was blinded by your choice of the darkness? Have you ever believed and heard from God but because of the state of your heart and mind, could not see God at work? Have you ever tried to fix the situation you found yourself in; thinking in your mind that you could do it better because you don't like the direction God was taking? We all find ourselves at various stages and in various experiences of faith. Where are you now? Where would you like to be?

The question of faith is one that is central to the Christmas season. How can we find real and lasting hope, joy and sparkle in something we don't actually believe in? How can we find meaning in the season when we lack faith in the message?

The message of Christmas begins with faith to hear the Voice of God, to surrender to the Voice of God and to praise Him for His Hand on our lives. The message of faith continues when we have faith that Christmas is the precursor to the Cross. Without Christmas, there is no Easter. Jesus' sacrifice on the Cross and His resurrection on the third day has guaranteed salvation for all who confess the Name of Jesus.

Christmas is not just about peace and joy but also points to the hope to come in the death and resurrection of our Lord; Christmas points to salvation. The real meaning of Christmas is not found in material gifts but in the ultimate gift given to us by Jesus; reconciliation, repair of the damaged relationship and restoration of our eternal walk with the Father.

If you have faith to believe the intended message of Christmas and make that your focus this Christmas season, I guarantee you that you will discover the longer-lasting truths about Christmas. The truths that will hold it all together; not just while the shops and stations play Christmas music and the stores have sales, but the truths that will hold it all together and make it applicable in our daily lives long into the days, weeks and months of the next year.

Thank you so much for coming on this journey of Christmas as a season of faith with me. I hope that it has led you to think about your faith and about Christmas in a new and different light; a light that has helped to bring back the sparkle of the season.

May the Lord Bless you and yours this Christmas Season and may His Hand of Blessing extend into the New Year, as you seek to learn and live by faith in the Lord Jesus Christ as Savior. And as you continue to rejoice in and worship Almighty God!

Let us pray together:

Heavenly Father, Almighty God, we come before You once again and praise Your Holy Name. We thank You for this journey through Christmas as a season of faith. We thank You for the opportunity to fellowship together through these devotions; the opportunity to seek Your Voice and Your will for our lives and the opportunity to see Christmas as a lifelong event, not just a season dictated by retail and media, that leaves us burned out and deflated on the 26th of December. We know that You have a much greater plan and purpose for our lives. We understand that You sent Your Beloved Son to earth in the form of a Child for a much greater purpose than gifts and glitter; that you sent Him that He would live as a man and be sacrificed on the cross, rising again on the third day, to cover our sins and grant us eternal life and an eternal walk with you! We ask for Your guidance and direction, Father, as we seek to understand faith and how it impacts our lives and our decisions and our walk with You. Grant us wisdom and understanding. I ask, Father, that You bless each and everyone reading these devotions – their families, friends, homes and lives. That You would show each and every one of them that You loved them enough to send Your one and only Son to die for their sins; that they just need to believe and confess with their mouth that they are in need of a Savior, that Jesus is that Savior and that they want Him to be Lord of their life. " The word is near you, in your mouth and in your heart' [that is, the word of faith that we preach] that if you confess with our mouth the Lord Jesus and believe in your heart that God has raised Him from the dead, you will be saved. For with the heart one believes unto righteousness, and with the mouth confession is made unto salvation." Romans 10:8-10. We pray all of these things in the precious Name of Jesus. Amen and Amen and Amen.

APPENDIX

MEANING IN THE SEASON THROUGH FAITH IN THE MESSAGE FOR SMALL GROUPS

Based on: Advent Devotions to Take You Deeper
Laurie Hopkins

Timeline: 6 Weeks

Summary:

The Christmas season is rapidly approaching. People are already counting down the days until they can begin decorating and others are already making plans for celebrations and activities. People are making preparations for the season. What better way to prepare for the season than by spending 6 weeks discussing the Meaning in the Season by looking at the Faith in the Message. We often plan ahead by shopping early, organizing celebrations and activities and by making lots of lists. But how often do we take the time to sit and examine our hearts? For many of us, Christmas has lost its sparkle. We get bogged down in the busyness, the excess and the time commitment. And by the end of it, we are ready for it to be over. What if this year, we were able to find the basic truths that will hold it all together; not just while the shops and stations play Christmas music and the stores have sales, but the truths that will hold it all together and make it applicable in our daily lives long into the days, weeks and months of the next year? Join us as we explore Christmas as a Season of Faith. Come ready to have a lovely time of fellowship and honest conversations about our relationship with Christmas.

Week 1

A Thread of Faith

Reading: Introduction

1. The introduction begins with the following statement: "The Christmas season is upon us once again. We like to see it come and inevitably, by the end of it, we love to see it go." How true is this for you?

2. The following 3 are given as examples of some of the things we tire off in the season. Talk about your response to each of them throughout the season:

Busyness

Excess

Time commitment

3. Has Christmas lost its sparkle for you? If you start strong, do you feel by the end of the season that you have had enough?

4. Are you ready to "look a little closer, dig a little deeper, and bring out longer-lasting truths about the Christmas season"?

5. What do you see as some of the most important "truths" of Christmas?

6. If someone didn't know anything about the meaning of Christmas, would these "truths" be obvious to them in the things you and your family do throughout the season?

7. How do you understand this statement: "There can be no Easter without Christmas."

8. How would you define faith?

9. Have you ever considered "faith" as a thread that runs throughout the Christmas message?

What kinds of faith do you think about when you think about Christmas?

10. How does your faith impact your celebration of Christmas?

11. Do you have faith in the truth of the birth of the Christ Child?

12. Do you have faith in the hope that that birth brings forth?

Cue Care Question: What sparkle are you hoping to bring back to the Christmas season this year? What might that look like for you?

Week 2

Sign or Surrender

Reading: Chapter 1

1. What do we know about Zacharias' background? (Luke 1:5-7; Luke 1:9). What do we know about Mary's background? (Luke 1:27) How are they similar? How are they different?

2. What do we know about the message Zacharias received? (Luke 1:13-17). What do we know about the message Mary received? (Luke 1:28; Luke 1:30-33, 35-37). How are they similar? How are they different?

3. What do we know about Zacharias' response to the message? (Luke 1:12; Luke 1:18-20). What do we know about Mary's response to the message? (Luke 1:29, 34, 38). How are they similar? How are they different?

4. What did the message require of Zacharias? What did the message require of Mary?

5. How would you describe Zacharias' faith? How would you describe Mary's faith?

6. In what way is your own faith like Zacharias'? In what way is your faith like Mary's?

7. In what way has your faith cost you? In what circumstances have you asked the Lord for a sign?

Cue Care Question: What is the Lord asking you to believe and/or do, in faith, this Christmas season?

Week 3

Senses and Serving

Reading: Chapter 2

1. Have you had any "aha" moments so far?

Hearing
2. What do we know about Joseph?
3. Joseph heard from God on 4 different occasions. (Matthew 1:20, Matthew 2:13, 20, 22). What were the messages and what was his response each time?
4. John 10:27 says, "My sheep hear My voice, and I know them, and they follow me." How do you hear the voice of God?
5. What can we say about Joseph's faith?

Praising
6. What did Elizabeth do once she had conceived? (Luke 1:24-25) Do you get the impression from the text that she praised the Lord, rather than questioning the Lord during her "set aside" time?
7. Psalm 23:3 says, "But You are holy, enthroned in the praises of Israel." The Hebrew word for enthroned is yashab, pronounced yä·shav'. It is defined this way: to dwell, remain, sit, abide, to inhabit. What does this mean to you?
8. What happened when Mary went to visit Elizabeth? (Luke 1:41-25)
9. What can we say about Elizabeth's faith?

Seeing is believing
10. What do we know about Simeon? (Luke 2:27-32)
11. What can we say about Simeon's faith?
12. How does Simeon's faith parallel Abraham's faith? (Genesis 13: 14-17; Hebrews 11:13)

Serving

13. What do we know about Anna? (Luke 2:37, 38)

14. What can we say about Anna's faith?

Cue Card Question: In this chapter, we read about 4 different kinds of faith:

Faith that hears and obeys

Faith that accepts and praises

Faith that waits on the promise in everyday life

Faith that serves as it waits

Where is your faith this Christmas season? In which of these 4 areas would you like to increase your faith?

Week 4

Faith and Sight

Reading: Chapter 3

Do You See What I See?

1. What message did the shepherds receive? (Luke 2: 13-14)
2. What was the shepherds' reaction to the message? (Luke 2:15)
3. How did they respond to seeing the Baby? (Luke 2: 17, 20)
4. How can we describe the faith of the shepherds?

Do You Know What I Know?

5. Who were the wise men?
6. What led them to Bethlehem?
7. What was their faith based on?
8. How did their faith require commitment?
9. What did they do when they found the Baby?

Blinded by the Darkness

10. Matthew 2:3 tells us that following the query of the wise men, "Herod the king....was troubled, and all Jerusalem with

him." It seems obvious that Herod would be troubled, but why do you think the chief priests and scribes would also be troubled?

11. The chief priests and scribes knew the prophecy, but didn't seem excited by it? They demonstrated belief but not faith. What do you think is the difference? Faith = (Belief × Action × Confidence)
12. John 3 tells us that when the Light came into the world that men loved darkness because their deeds were evil, and therefore they hid from the light. How do you think this may apply to the reaction of the chief priests and scribes?

Self-Faith
13. Did Herod have faith? Or belief?
14. What are some other terms we use to describe self-faith?
15. In this chapter we read about 4 different kinds of faith:

> Faith that sees, hears and seeks more
> Faith that commits upon knowing
> Faith/belief that hides from the light
> Faith/belief in self

Cue Card Question: What lessons can you learn from the Shepherds and the Wisemen and their faith? How can you seek more and share more of the Saviour during this Christmas Season? You know the Baby is Jesus, your Saviour, how can you show more commitment to Him and His work this Christmas season?

Week 5

The Meaning in the Message

Reading: Chapter 4

1. In thinking about the different kinds of faith we have discussed, whose faith do you identify most with right now? Whose faith would you like to identify most with right now?

2. "The question of faith is one that is central to the Christmas season. How can we find real and lasting hope, joy and sparkle in something we don't actually believe in? How can we find meaning in the season when we lack faith in the message?"
How do you feel about this statement?

3. Perhaps the above statement isn't an issue for us because we have faith in the message. How can we help those around us to find faith in that message so they do can find meaning in the season?

4. The intention of this devotional was to "look a little deeper, and bring out longer-lasting truths about the Christmas season." To "strip down the complexities and find the basic truths that will hold it all together; not just while the shops and stations play Christmas music and the stores have sales, but the truths that will hold it all together and make it applicable in our daily lives long in to the days, weeks and months of the next year."
What will you take away from this devotional study that will help put the sparkle back in your own Christmas? What will you take away from this devotional study that will help put the sparkle back in the Christmas of those around you?

Cue Card Question: What is one response you can have prepared to answer someone this Christmas when they comment that "Christmas is not what it used to be" or "Christmas has lost its sparkle" or "I wish that Christmas felt the same as it used to"?

Week 6

Putting it all Together

Facilitator's Directions:

Each week's study ends with a "Cue Card Question" designed to encourage self-reflection. Give each participant a blank cue card and ask them to answer the "Cue Card Question". They are not required to share this with the group (although some may wish to discuss). Have the participant place in their envelope to save for the remaining weeks of the study.

In Week 6 the group will spend some time looking at their 5 Weeks of Cue Card Questions and creating a "visual" representation of what they have reflected on during this time. In Week 6 provide the group with:
- 2 blank pieces of heavier paper or Bristol Board (If you are creative you can create a template for the group with 5 separate areas on that one piece of paper to write in – if you are not feeling creative, they can work from a blank sheet).
-markers and pencil crayons or regular crayons and pens/pencils
-a clear sheet protector

Have the group follow the Participants Directions below. When they are done, they can put their papers back to back in the clear sheet protector. This will serve as a visual reminder of their self-reflection during the study and some concrete actionable items for them to work on through the Christmas season.

Participants Directions:

Take all of your cue cards out of the envelope and take a few minutes to review the questions and your answers for each week.

Page 1

Create 5 blocks on your page. For each block, take one cue card and summarize what you **want to remember** in a few keywords or sentences.

For example, Week 1 Question was: What sparkle are you hoping to bring back to the Christmas season this year? What might that look like for you?

You may choose to write: SPARKLE, JOY, FEWER THINGS MORE PEOPLE

Page 2

Create 5 blocks on your page. For each block, take one cue care and write one very specific, concrete, thing that **you are going to do** this Christmas season related to the answer you provided for that week.

For example, Week 1 Question was: What sparkle are you hoping to bring back to the Christmas season this year? What might that look like for you?

You may choose to write: I will tell my friends that instead of gifts this year, I would rather plan a time to spend together and have tea and cookies and chat.

When you are done, you can put them back to back in the sleeve protector. You will take them home with you and look at them throughout the Christmas season to remind you of what we discussed, what you learned and what you heard from God during our time together.

I hope you have enjoyed the small group study. I would love your feedback. Be in touch by email at laurie@lauriehopkins.ca

ABOUT THE AUTHOR

Laurie Hopkins is a worshiper at heart and desires that all would learn the privilege and power of worship. She has had an extensive life journey in which the Lord has taught her to "dance in the valley"; which allows her to be a victorious overcomer no matter the circumstances. Laurie has a heart for the people of God; to see them healed and delivered and walking in the authentic and abundant life they have been called to. Laurie is a speaker and writer; she is also trained in Restoring the Foundations Ministry (Issue Focused Ministry) which seeks freedom and the building of solid foundations for the people of God. Laurie lives with her husband, John, in Porters Lake, Nova Scotia, Canada. You can find her on her blog/website at https://www.lauriehopkins.ca/ or on Facebook at https://www.facebook.com/GodsWritingDancer/

Made in the USA
Columbia, SC
19 December 2019